Buns and Bananas

Written by
Cath Jones

Illustrated by
Andy Hamilton

Iman and Akin set off for a picnic in the forest.

Iman took some buns and Akin took a big sandwich.

They kept the food in a backpack.

The pair got off the bus at the bus stop.

They set off down a trail into the forest.

There were lots of chimpanzees sitting in the treetops.

But Iman and Akin did not spot them!

Soon the pair were hot and worn out.

"Let us rest under that big kapok tree," Iman said.

But look! A chimpanzee was peeling bark off the kapok tree.

It hid when Iman and Akin sat down under it.

Akin took out the picnic.

The chimpanzee slid up to them.

But Akin and Iman still did not spot the chimpanzee!

"I will pick some bananas," said Iman.

But the bananas were much too high up in the treetops.

"Yum! I can smell buns!" said the chimpanzee to himself. "I like buns!"

The chimpanzee did a handstand.

"That is a big backpack. Is there food for me?" said the chimpanzee.

"Yes," said Iman and Akin.

But then … Gulp! MUNCH!

The chimpanzee fed on **all** the buns **and** the big sandwich!

"**BURP!** Thank you," said the chimpanzee. "That was a good picnic!"

Now Iman and Akin were sad.

There was no food left for them!

"You need some food too," said the chimpanzee. "So I will pick some bananas for you!"

Soon Akin, Iman and the chimpanzee had lots of bananas.